GLIMPSE

LONDON

ISBN: 978-1-951412-11-1

Manufactured in China.

Design by Laurie Nicoud and Analia Pribyl,
The Creative Clique.

10 9 8 7 6 5 4 3 2

THE
collective
BOOK STUDIO

Oakland, California
www.thecollectivebook.studio

BUTCHERS
14
Putney
FAGANS
BUS
STOP

luxury city guides

www.glimpseguides.com

@glimpseguides

Contents

01.

INTRODUCTION

LONDON

London is one of the most exuberant cities in the world, and among the best places to travel for cultural experiences. Its renowned museums and exhibitions, plays and musicals, high-end shopping and world-class hotels and restaurants provide endless itineraries, and we are so excited to launch our hardcover guides with London. We have listed the very best of the city, and we are delighted that this guide works for travelers of all ages, including those with children.

Jordan Rhodes launched Glimpse because she found a gap in the luxury family travel space, and while these guides work for solo travelers and couples, we have written them for families, as well. Jordan loves introducing the world to her little ones, and we hope these guides will make travel with your own a bit easier.

Be sure to check out our website glimpseguides.com for current events and updates in each city (especially as some recommendations may have closed). You can also follow us on Instagram @glimpseguides.

London Guide by Jordan Rhodes
Design by Laurie Nicoud and Analia Pribyl

Please download the corresponding Glimpse app in the app store for maps of London with our recommendations highlighted, directions, current weather, the ability to save your favorites, notes, and quick access to contact information to look up hours of operation.

If you would like help planning your trip, please reach out to Glimpse Founder Jordan Rhodes at Jordanr@brownelltravel.com. Jordan is an ambassador with Brownell Travel, one of the most prestigious Virtuoso-affiliated travel agencies in the world, and would love to help further curate your vacation.

GIVE A GLIMPSE

100% of this guide's profits goes to our charity Give A Glimpse, which gives underserved students the educational gift of travel, whether sponsorships for study abroad programs, travel funding for internships, or travel funding for volunteer opportunities.

At Glimpse, we believe that travel is one of the most important forms of education. It has the ability to enhance young minds through connection, independence, and responsibility. More importantly, travel can help develop cultural sensitivity, compassion, and a sense of wonder. We believe that all deserve those experiences.

By purchasing this guide or any products we sell on our website, or by hiring us to plan your vacations through our partnership with Brownell Travel agency, you too are helping Give A Glimpse.

CLEA
Give A Glimpse recipient in Rome, 2019

ACKNOWLEDGMENTS

A huge thank you to Waris Ahluwalia, Lily Aldridge, Taylor Angino, Carolyn Baring, Dean Burrell, Nicole Castiblanco Silva, Brenden Clark, Jasmine Contomichalos, Angela Engel, Becca W. Flanagan, Sophia Flores, Claiborne Swanson Frank, Rachel Cecil Gurney, Hannah Cecil Harden, Emma Hartland-Mahon, Ian Malone, Christiane Hill, Phebe Huth, Lucia Ruck Keene, Lauren Bush Lauren, Erdem Moralioglu, Laurie Nicoud, Barrett Norton, Roopal Patel, Laura Paterson, Analia Pribyl, Noah Rhodes, Nicki Rose, Glenn Shaw, Catherine Smith, Melinda Stevens, Heather K. Terry, Rebecca Thomson, Catherine Tompkins, Rosie van Cutsem, Esmeralda Veliz, Olivia Weiss, Khaki Wennstrom, Gucci Westman, Julia Wharton, and Anna Wintour.

02.

GUIDE TO THE GUIDE

Each recommendation lists the address, phone number, and website (if available) and gives a simple overview. For those traveling with children, we have listed whether a restaurant has high chairs and kids' menus. There are also a few words listed to sum up each restaurant, including the type of food served.

THE GUIDE TO THOSE WORDS:

CASUAL
Jeans and flats are appropriate here.

STYLISH
Your outfit should be smart and sophisticated.

POSH
Men, grab your coat and tie;
ladies, slip on your heels.

CLASSIC
The décor is conservative and elegant.

CONTEMPORARY
The décor is simple and modern.

CONTEMPORARY/CLASSIC
The décor contains elements of each.

RUSTIC
The décor is most likely a pub setting.

CONSTANT
The spot never goes out of style.

HOT
This is the place to be at the moment.

03.

RESTAURANTS

THE CONNAUGHT HOTEL

BY NEIGHBORHOOD

**Can be found in the Date Night section*

BALTHAZAR

Address: 4–6 Russell Street,
Covent Garden, WC2B 5HZ
Phone: 020 3301 1155
Website: balthazarlondon.com
Great for: BREAKFAST, LUNCH, AFTERNOON TEA, DINNER, WEEKEND BRUNCH

Every bit as chic as its New York City counterpart, Balthazar London is the perfect spot after sightseeing in the area. This Parisian café is just a stone's throw from the Covent Garden market, with a brilliant menu and stylish clientele. Plus who doesn't love a classic French restaurant, especially by restaurateur Keith McNally?

FRENCH | CLASSIC | HOT | STYLISH
HIGH CHAIRS | CHILDREN'S MENU

BERNERS TAVERN

Address: 10 Berners Street,
Fitzrovia, W1T 3NP
Phone: 020 7908 7979
Website: bernerstavern.com
Great for: BREAKFAST, LUNCH, DINNER, WEEKEND BRUNCH

Berners Tavern in Ian Schrager's London Edition hotel is one of the most visually stunning sights in the city. Massive ceilings with ornate moldings and large gilded chandeliers converge with walls covered in oil paintings and photographs, completing the feel of a glamorous, bygone era. The room is so spacious and the crowd is so loud that no one will mind kids lining the banquettes.

BRITISH | CLASSIC | HOT | STYLISH
HIGH CHAIRS | CHILDREN'S MENU

“

LONDON IS ENCHANTING.

I STEP UPON A TAWNY

COLOURED MAGIC CARPET,

IT SEEMS, AND GET CARRIED

INTO BEAUTY WITHOUT

RAISING A FINGER.

Virginia Woolf

CECCONI'S MAYFAIR

Address:
5A Burlington Gardens,
Mayfair, W1S 3EP
Phone:
020 7434 1500
Website:
cecconis.co.uk
Great for:
BREAKFAST, LUNCH, DINNER,
WEEKEND BRUNCH

No matter what, we always head straight to Cecconi's after an international flight. There's just something about the beautiful marble interior with green leather seating and flowing cappuccinos that start our London trips off right. Plus the large open windows in bustling Mayfair provide great people watching as we make plans for the day.

ITALIAN | CLASSIC | CONSTANT | STYLISH
HIGH CHAIRS

COLBERT

Address: 50–52 Sloane Square,
Chelsea, SW1W 8AX
Phone: 020 7730 2804
Website: colbertchelsea.com
Great for: BREAKFAST, LUNCH, DINNER

This French-inspired café right on Sloane Square is one of our favorite spots for a casual yet elegant meal with the kids. You will definitely feel like a resident among all the locals. Afterward pop across the street to the Saatchi Gallery for an exhibit, walk along the King's Road and do some shopping, or wander through Belgravia admiring the gorgeous old homes.

ITALIAN | CLASSIC | CONSTANT
STYLISH | HIGH CHAIRS

DAPHNE'S

Address: 112 Draycott Avenue,
Chelsea, SW3 3AE
Phone: 020 7589 4257
Website: daphnes-restaurant.co.uk
Great for: LUNCH, DINNER

Another absolutely chic spot is Daphne's, which is by the same restaurant group as Scott's and The Ivy, so of course one can expect perfection. The conservatory seating is cozy in colder months and blissful in warmer months, and the glamorous bar is the perfect meeting place after a day of shopping in Chelsea. Bustling and exciting, the atmosphere is fine for kids.

ITALIAN | CLASSIC | CONSTANT
STYLISH | HIGH CHAIRS

A GLIMPSE

There are over 300 languages spoken in London.

The most popular languages after English are Bengali, Gujarati, Punjabi, Cantonese, and Mandarin.

DININGS SW3

Address:
Lennox Gardens Mews,
Chelsea, SW3 2JH
Phone:
020 7723 0666
Website:
dinings.co.uk
Great for:
LUNCH, DINNER

Arguably some of the best Japanese food in London can be found at Dinings, with some of the freshest sushi and sashimi in the city. Located in a charming mews building in Chelsea, the contemporary space is bursting with energy and is one of our favorite stops after wandering around the neighborhood.

JAPANESE | CLASSIC | CONSTANT | STYLISH
KIDS ALLOWED AT LUNCH BUT MUST BE OVER AGE FIVE AT DINNER

DINNER

Address: 66 Knightsbridge,
Knightsbridge, SW1X 7LA
Phone: 020 7201 3833
Website: dinnerbyheston.co.uk
Great for: LUNCH, DINNER

Even though it has been open for many years now, Heston Blumenthal's renowned restaurant at the Mandarin Oriental in Knightsbridge is still one of the hottest spots in London. Inspired by historic British gastronomy, the menu has received two Michelin stars, and self-proclaimed foodies declare this at the top of their dining list. While children over four are welcome and high chairs are available, lunchtime would be a better option with kids.

BRITISH | CONTEMPORARY | HOT
STYLISH | HIGH CHAIRS

FORTNUM & MASON DIAMOND JUBILEE TEA SALON

Address: 181 Piccadilly,
St. James's, W1A 1ER
Phone: 020 7734 8040
Website: fortnumandmason.com
Great for: LUNCH, AFTERNOON TEA

If it's good enough for the queen, it's more than good enough for us. The luxury department store has sold tea for over 300 years, making this the ultimate place to enjoy afternoon tea. "Tearistas" are on hand to conduct tastings on the 82 different blends available, and the salon is a very civilized way to enjoy a British tradition. Don't leave without one of their famous food hampers.

TEA | CLASSIC | CONSTANT | STYLISH
HIGH CHAIRS | CHILDREN'S MENU

“

THE MAN WHO

CAN DOMINATE A

LONDON DINNER-TABLE

CAN DOMINATE

THE WORLD.

Oscar Wilde

FRANCO MANCA

Address: 111 Westbourne Grove,
Westbourne Grove, W2 4UW
Phone: 020 3026 6305
Website: francomanca.co.uk
Great for: LUNCH, DINNER

When your stylish London friends tell you this is where they take their kids for casual pizza, you go there, too, especially when it's made out of slow-rise sourdough bread. The rustic, brick-exposed interior means you don't have to worry about the kids ruining anything, and the daily-changing specials always hit the mark.

PIZZA | RUSTIC | CONSTANT | CASUAL
HIGH CHAIRS | CHILDREN'S MENU

GRANGER & CO

Address: 175 Westbourne Grove,
Notting Hill, W11 2SB
Phone: 020 7229 9111
Website: grangerandco.com
Great for: BREAKFAST, LUNCH, DINNER

This casual Notting Hill hotspot, by famed Australian chef and TV star Bill Granger, is a requirement for anyone in the area. The menu, full of dishes made from fresh, local produce, has a decidedly simple flare, with the wine list adding a nice sophisticated touch. While it is kid-friendly, reservations cannot be made and it operates on a first come, first served basis, so heading over for an early lunch or dinner would be best.

AUSTRALIAN | CONTEMPORARY | CONSTANT
CASUAL | HIGH CHAIRS | THREE OPTIONS FOR KIDS

A GLIMPSE

Jimi Hendrix lived at 23 Brook Street, which has been used as offices but is now being converted into a museum.

Two doors down at 25 Brook Street is where the famous composer Handel lived from 1723 until his death in 1759.

GYMKHANA

Address:
42 Albemarle Street,
Mayfair, W1S 4JH
Phone:
020 3011 5900
Website:
gymkhanalondon.com
Great for:
LUNCH, DINNER

Perhaps consistently the most popular Indian spot for those visiting London, Gymkhana creates truly incredible food in a sophisticated – yet lively – setting. On date night, plan to stay a while at the bar, and if you have a large group, check out the beautiful, private banquettes down in the vault, which are also a good option if you really want to bring the kids.

INDIAN | CLASSIC | CONSTANT | POSH
HIGH CHAIRS

HAKKASAN MAYFAIR

Address:
17 Bruton Street,
Mayfair, W1J 6QB
Phone:
020 7907 1888
Website:
hakkasan.com
Great for:
LUNCH, DINNER

One of the most popular choices for Asian cuisine in London, Hakkasan is also a top pick because of its sleek interior and energetic vibe. The fashion crowd, business crowd, tourists, and locals all converge to enjoy the innovative Cantonese dishes, which have received a coveted Michelin star. Although there is no children's menu, there are plenty of options to choose from and a good chance the kids will be enchanted by the lively atmosphere.

CHINESE | CONTEMPORARY | CONSTANT
STYLISH

HARRY'S DOLCE VITA

Address: 27–31, Basil Street,
Knightsbridge, SW3 1BB
Phone: 020 3940 1020
Website: harrysdolcevita.com
Great for: BREAKFAST, LUNCH, DINNER, WEEKEND BRUNCH

This is one of our favorite spots for a meal in London, for many reasons. First of all, it's in a cute section of Knightsbridge, and we love walking around before and after a meal. It's also part of the Caprice Holdings Group, which owns Scott's and The Ivy, so you know you'll get a great meal and excellent service. Finally, we love that lots of locals seem to always be here, which makes us feel as if we live in the neighborhood.

ITALIAN | CLASSIC | CONSTANT | STYLISH
HIGH CHAIRS | CHILDREN'S MENU

HÉLÈNE DARROZE

Address: Carlos Place,
Mayfair, W1K 2AL
The Connaught Hotel
Phone: 020 3147 7200
Website: the-connaught.co.uk
Great for: LUNCH, DINNER

Located in The Connaught hotel, Hélène Darroze is formal dining without the stuffiness. The hotel is one of our favorites in the world. It's the perfect spot for a special occasion in a gorgeous setting, but keep in mind that only children ages seven and up are allowed.

FRENCH | CLASSIC | CONSTANT | POSH
THREE COURSES FOR KIDS

A GLIMPSE

The sandwich was invented in 1762 in England by the Earl of Sandwich, an aristocrat and gambler who did not want to put his cards down to eat, so he asked for his meat between slices of bread.

ISABEL

Address:
26 Albemarle Street,
Mayfair, W1S 4HY
Phone:
020 3096 9292
Website: isabelw1.london
Great for:
BREAKFAST, LUNCH, DINNER

Who wouldn't want to dine in a restaurant with de Gournay-clad bathroom walls and a gold-accented bar in the center of the room? Isabel is a true experience in the heart of Mayfair, brought to you by the same owner as Casa Cruz, so you know the Argentine fare is going to be amazing. Feel free to bring the kids for breakfast or lunch, but it is 18 and over after 6pm, and lots of diners stay for drinks in the club downstairs.

ARGENTINIAN | CONTEMPORARY/CLASSIC
CONSTANT | STYLISH

J SHEEKEY

Address:
28–32 Saint Martin's Court,
Covent Garden, WC2N 4AL
Phone:
020 7240 2565
Website:
j-sheekey.co.uk
Great for:
LUNCH, DINNER

Not many eateries have the honor of staying relevant for multiple years, much less for over a century. Since the 1890s J Sheekey has been the top fish restaurant in London, attracting celebrities, socialites, and seafood lovers. The impressive art collection and leather banquettes are aesthetically pleasing, and it's great for pre- and post-theater meals.

SEAFOOD | CLASSIC | CONSTANT
STYLISH | HIGH CHAIRS

KETTNER'S TOWNHOUSE

Address: 29 Romilly Street,
Soho, W1D 5HP
Phone: 020 7734 5650
Website: kettners.com
Great for: BREAKFAST, LUNCH, DINNER, WEEKEND BRUNCH

This Soho House spot is one of our go-tos for pre- and post-theater meals, as it's in the heart of the theater district. The 1920s design set across seven townhouses is always packed, and our personal favorite room is the champagne bar. Because it's a Soho House property expect to see some famous faces, and bonus–it is also a hotel.

SEAFOOD | CLASSIC | CONSTANT
STYLISH | HIGH CHAIRS

LA FAMIGLIA

Address: 7 Langton Street,
Chelsea, SW10 0JL
Phone: 020 7351 0761
Website: lafamiglia.co.uk
Great for: LUNCH, DINNER

Another classic neighborhood spot for perfect Italian food is La Famiglia, and once again, this is where our cool friends go with their kids for a good meal. Open for over 35 years, we love the black-and-white photos on the walls, and the terrace for warmer weather.

ITALIAN | CLASSIC | CONSTANT | STYLISH
HIGH CHAIRS | CHILDREN'S MENU

“

IN LONDON,

LOVE AND SCANDAL

ARE CONSIDERED THE

BEST SWEETENERS

OF TEA.

John Osborne

LA PETITE MAISON

Address: 53–54 Brook's Mews,
Mayfair, W1K 4EG
Phone: 020 7495 4774
Website: lpmlondon.co.uk
Great for: LUNCH, DINNER

For those who love the glamour of the south of France, La Petite Maison is the closest you'll come to finding it in London. With its airy, light-filled dining room in Mayfair, and French-Mediterranean dishes that are meant for sharing, the restaurant is always packed. Children are welcome, but keep it to lunchtime. We personally prefer coming here for date night, so we can enjoy one of the many selections of rosé from the gorgeous bar.

FRENCH | CLASSIC | CONSTANT | STYLISH
HIGH CHAIRS

NO. FIFTY CHEYNE

Address: 50 Cheyne Walk,
Chelsea, SW3 5LR
Phone: 020 7376 8787
Website: fiftycheyne.com
Great for: LUNCH, AFTERNOON TEA,
DINNER, WEEKEND BRUNCH

Situated in a gorgeous, recently renovated space with a creative French menu, No. Fifty Cheyne (formerly known as Cheyne Walk Brasserie) has a large following in London's Chelsea neighborhood. The elegant diners meet for animated conversations over lunch and dinner, and with private rooms and party spaces upstairs, it is the perfect place for an upscale meal with children, followed by a stroll through the picturesque surrounding streets near the Thames.

FRENCH | CLASSIC | CONSTANT | STYLISH
HIGH CHAIRS | CHILDREN'S MENU (AT LUNCH)

A GLIMPSE

Brits drink more than 163 million cups of tea everyday.

PIZZA EAST

Address: 310 Portobello Road,
Notting Hill, W10 5TA
Phone: 020 8969 4500
Website: pizzaeast.com
Great for: LUNCH, DINNER, WEEKEND BRUNCH

This is where stylish Notting Hill locals go for casual yet delicious pizza, and it's perfect for kids who are a little rowdy. Enjoy the rustic setting with wood-burning oven, followed by a walk around the neighborhood.

PIZZA | RUSTIC | CONSTANT | STYLISH
HIGH CHAIRS | CHILDREN'S MENU

ROKA

Address: 30 N Audley Street,
Mayfair, W1K 6ZF
Phone: 020 7305 5644
Website: rokarestaurant.com
Great for: LUNCH, DINNER

Part of the famous Zuma restaurant group, Roka now has several locations, as this restaurant chain continues to explode in popularity. The stark setting with tan wood is very typical of a contemporary Japanese restaurant, and the informal air is perfect for diners with children. Be sure to try the tasting menu if time allows.

JAPANESE | CONTEMPORARY | HOT | STYLISH

“

TRAVEL AND CHANGE

OF PLACE IMPART NEW VIGOR

TO THE MIND.

Seneca

SCOTT'S

Address:
20 Mount Street,
Mayfair, W1K 2HE
Phone:
020 7495 7309
Website:
scotts-restaurant.com
Great for:
LUNCH, DINNER

Scott's on Mount Street is the perfect stop after a day of shopping at the plethora of nearby designer stores. The loyal, upscale clientele is one reason why this restaurant has been popular for so many years. Other reasons include the amazing seafood and gorgeous champagne bar, as well as the management, who also run top spots J Sheekey, The Ivy, and Sexy Fish. In the summer, nothing is better than the sidewalk seating.

SEAFOOD | CLASSIC | CONSTANT
STYLISH | HIGH CHAIRS

SKETCH

Address: 9 Conduit Street,
Mayfair, W1S 2XG
Phone: 020 7659 4500
Website: sketch.london
Great for: LUNCH, AFTERNOON TEA, DINNER

Definitely the most instagrammed restaurant in London, Sketch is known for its pink décor and walls in The Gallery, which allows kids, and for its futuristic pods in the bathroom. Choose between the Alice in Wonderland–like afternoon tea and dinner for your meal, but keep in mind that this is a very popular spot, so you may need to book in advance. The Lecture Room and Library has been awarded three Michelin stars, and children under six are not allowed.

BRITISH | CONTEMPORARY | CONSTANT
STYLISH | HIGH CHAIRS | KIDS' MENUS

THE ARCHDUKE

Address: Concert Hall Approach,
Southbank, SE1 8XU
Phone: 020 7928 9370
Website: blackandbluerestaurants.com
Great for: LUNCH, DINNER

If you're into music, steak, and wine, this is the spot for you. Featuring jazz every night and Sunday afternoons, it is a great spot to unwind after a day at the aquarium or London Eye, and was the first wine bar to open on the Southbank. Visitors will love the Scottish steaks and burgers, and kids will love the location under Waterloo's railway arches. Bonus: If this spot is too crowded, check out nearby sister restaurant, Waterloo, at 1 Mepham Street.

MODERN AMERICAN | CONTEMPORARY/CLASSIC
CONSTANT | CASUAL

THE ARCHDUKE

A GLIMPSE

Underneath Cleopatra's Needle on the Embankment, there's a time capsule from 1878 that's said to contain cigars, a razor, a portrait of Queen Victoria, copies of ten daily newspapers, and pictures of twelve "English beauties of the day."

THE IVY

Address:
1–5 West Street,
West End, WC2H 9NQ
Phone:
020 7836 4751
Website:
the-ivy.co.uk
Great for:
LUNCH, DINNER

With its recent well-publicized revamp, The Ivy's popularity has resurged and is now better than it was before, if that's possible. The famous spot has been known to welcome all kinds of celebrities, politicians, and royals, who appreciate its discreet dining room, dark windows, and playful reputation. It's also one of our go-tos for pre-theater dining.

BRITISH | CLASSIC | CONSTANT | STYLISH

THE IVY CHELSEA GARDEN

Address:
195–197 King's Road,
Chelsea, SW3 5EQ
Phone:
020 3301 0300
Website:
theivychelseagarden.com
Great for:
BREAKFAST, LUNCH, AFTERNOON TEA,
DINNER, WEEKEND BRUNCH

For a truly stylish dining experience, be sure to visit The Ivy Chelsea Garden for lunch or an early dinner. The fashion crowd loves this spot, and we personally love the gorgeous garden seating, fireplace, and atrium full of flowers. Afterward, enjoy some great shopping in the area.

BRITISH | CLASSIC | CONSTANT | STYLISH
HIGH CHAIRS

THE RIVER CAFÉ

Address:
Thames Wharf, Rainville Road,
Hammersmith,W6 9HA
Phone:
020 7386 4200
Website:
rivercafe.co.uk
Great for:
LUNCH, DINNER

Described by many as the best Italian food in London, The River Café in Hammersmith along the River Thames provides a gorgeous setting, whether having a romantic dinner with your significant other or enjoying brunch with the entire family. The indoor dining area gives off a somewhat industrial vibe, albeit charming and exciting, while the outdoor seating is very pleasant, but packed, during warmer months. We love the grassy area outside, and it's a perfect place for the kids to run around before the food arrives.

ITALIAN | CONTEMPORARY | CONSTANT
STYLISH | HIGH CHAIRS | CHILDREN'S MENU

THE WOLSELEY

Address:
160 Piccadilly,
St. James's, W1J 9EB
Phone:
020 7499 6996
Website:
thewolseley.com
Great for:
BREAKFAST, LUNCH,
AFTERNOON TEA, DINNER

It is no secret in London that The Wolseley is a favorite of locals and tourists. While best known for its famous breakfast, lunch and dinner are just as packed, and there is a constant excitement buzzing throughout the day. The grand two-story dining area with contemporary chandeliers in the light-filled atrium is a stunning sight.

BRITISH | CONTEMPORARY/CLASSIC | CONSTANT STYLISH | HIGH CHAIRS

WAGAMAMA

Address: 5 Cardinal Walk,
Roof Garden Level, Victoria, SW1E 5JE
Phone: 020 7828 0561
Website: wagamama.com
Great for: LUNCH, DINNER

While this seems to be more of an American favorite and not typically the kind of restaurant we have in our guides, we think every family should make a trip to Wagamama when visiting the U.K. The casual chain serves Japanese dishes in a fast-paced, family-style environment, and we love to go to this location near Buckingham Palace for an early meal after landing from an overnight flight, mainly because there is a big outdoor area to run around on.

JAPANESE | CONTEMPORARY | CONSTANT
CASUAL | HIGH CHAIRS | CHILDREN'S MENU

ZUMA

Address: 5 Raphael Street,
Knightsbridge, SW7 1DL
Phone: 020 7584 1010
Website: zumarestaurant.com
Great for: LUNCH, DINNER

In the center of fashionable Knightsbridge lies Zuma, a highly popular Japanese hotspot with some of the best sushi around. Glamorous tourists and local residents congregate around the swanky bar, then proceed to their tables to rave over dishes such as the thinly sliced sea bass with yuzu and truffle oil or the famous spicy tuna roll. Parents rejoice: There is also a kids menu.

JAPANESE | CONTEMPORARY | CONSTANT
STYLISH | HIGH CHAIRS

“

I LIKE THE SPIRIT

OF THIS GREAT LONDON

WHICH I FEEL AROUND ME.

Charlotte Bronte

04.

DATE NIGHT

CASA CRUZ

Address: 123A Clarendon Road,
Notting Hill, W11 4JG
Phone: 020 3321 5400
Website: casacruz.london.com
Great for: LUNCH, DINNER

Moody vibes are on hand at this dark, Argentinean eatery in Notting Hill, and the sophisticated West London crowd loves it. Come for the South American–influenced dishes and stay all night for the loud music and after-hours revelery on the smoking patio.

ARGENTINEAN | CLASSIC | HOT | STYLISH

CHILTERN FIREHOUSE

Address: 1 Chiltern Street,
Marylebone, W1U 7PA
Phone: 020 7073 7676
Website: chilternfirehouse.com
Great for: BREAKFAST, BRUNCH, LUNCH, DINNER

The popular restaurant at Chiltern Firehouse, André Balazs's first London hotel, immediately established itself as the hottest scene in town when it opened a few years ago. Located in Marylebone in an old fire station, the outdoor terrace is coveted in warmer months, and the party is always going strong.

AMERICAN | CONTEMPORARY/CLASSIC
HOT | STYLISH

"

BLESSED ARE THE CURIOUS,

FOR THEY SHALL HAVE

ADVENTURES.

Lovelle Drachman

CORE BY CLARE SMYTH

Address:
92 Kensington Park Road,
Notting Hill, W11 2PN
Phone:
020 3937 5086
Website:
coreby claresmyth.com
Great for:
LUNCH, DINNER

This is hands down our favorite fine-dining spot in London, although you will not find any stuffiness here. Clare Smyth is a genius, and her two Michelin stars plus weeks-long waitlist for a reservation proves it.

BRITISH | CLASSIC | HOT | STYLISH

JAMAVAR

Address: 8 Mount Street,
Mayfair, W1K 3NF
Phone: 020 7499 1800
Website: jamavarrestaurants.com
Great for: LUNCH, DINNER

When we're in London without our kids (which is typically once a month), we always try to squeeze in a visit to Jamavar for dinner. Not only do they make some of the best Indian food we've ever had, it is the most gorgeous setting in Mayfair, and is within walking distance of many of our favorite hotels.

INDIAN | CLASSIC | HOT | POSH | HIGH CHAIRS
CHILDREN'S MENU (AT LUNCH)

KITTY FISHER'S

Address: 10 Shepherd Market,
Mayfair, W1J 7QF
Phone: 020 3302 1661
Website: kittyfishers.com
Great for: LUNCH, DINNER

Want an experience that is posh, cozy, fun, and hard to get into? Then Kitty Fisher's should be at the top of the list. Located in an area that was once London's red-light district, they play off of that theme with their intimate atmosphere and sexy vibes. Expect to see a famous face here.

MODERN BRITISH | CLASSIC | CONSTANT
STYLISH

JAMAVAR

A GLIMPSE

At Wimbledon, more than 275,000 glasses of Pimm's and more than 190,000 strawberries are consumed.

PARK CHINOIS

Address: 17 Berkeley Street,
Mayfair, W1J 8EA
Phone: 020 3327 8888
Website: parkchinois.com
Great for: LUNCH, DINNER

Step back in time to 1930s Shanghai at this exciting, decadent Chinese restaurant in Mayfair. Enjoy an upscale meal with your significant other surrounded by posh patrons and gold and red accents while listening to crooners take the stage with songs from past eras. Don't be afraid to head to the dance floor after an unforgettable dinner.

CHINESE | CLASSIC | CONSTANT | POSH

WILTON'S

Address: 55 Jermyn Street,
St. James's, SW1Y 6LX
Phone: 020 7629 9955
Website: wiltons.co.uk
Great for: LUNCH, DINNER

Established in 1742, Wilton's is fine dining at its English best. The furnishings are a great combination of old and new, with white tablecloths and velvet chairs, while both portraits and contemporary art adorn the walls. Entrées consist mainly of game and fish, and patrons love the oyster bar. Our preppy friends love this spot.

BRITISH | CLASSIC | CONSTANT | POSH

“

YOU LEARN A LOT ABOUT

SOMEONE WHEN YOU SHARE

A MEAL TOGETHER.

Anthony Bourdain

05.

HOTELS

CLARIDGE'S

Address:
49 Brook Street,
Mayfair, W1K 4HR
Phone:
020 7629 8860
Website:
claridges.co.uk

Quite possibly the most famous of all London hotels, Claridge's has an unrivaled historic past and an art deco interior unlike any other in the city. The black-and-white marble floor at the foot of the sweeping staircase has welcomed a plethora of famous faces over the last 150-plus years, including everyone from Queen Elizabeth and Jackie Onassis to Anna Wintour and Diane von Furstenberg. The rooms and suites each have their own unique styles and luxurious Bamford bath products, while the signature designer suites are known for their ornate furnishings and personal butlers. Children are treated like royalty, and no one will want to leave. The location in Mayfair is a perfect starting point for the best the city has to offer.

“

NOT THAT I INTEND TO DIE, BUT WHEN I DO, I DON'T WANT TO GO TO HEAVEN—I WANT TO GO TO CLARIDGE'S.

Spencer Tracy

NUMBER SIXTEEN

Address:
16 Sumner Place,
South Kensington, SW7 3EG
Phone:
020 7589 5232
Website:
firmdalehotels.com

For those families looking for a hotel that feels like a house, this is the one for you. Number Sixteen is a charming boutique hotel by the Firmdale group, also responsible for eight other London properties. This location is known for being very quaint, and families will love strolling down the quiet streets of residential South Kensington while popping into the many casual restaurants and shops. Rooms are individually decorated in owner and designer Kit Kemp's quirky yet charming style and come with all the amenities expected of a top tier hotel. Children will love the welcome gift upon arrival, the selection of games and activities, and the milk and cookies at bedtime. Adults will enjoy afternoon tea in the beautiful garden on a sunny day, although with all the wonderful attractions in the area, like the Victoria and Albert and Natural History museums just steps away, we recommend venturing out. Our only concern is that there are lots of stairs, so it may be a bit of a challenge for those with strollers. Other than that, be prepared to feel right at home.

A GLIMPSE

Oscar Wilde was once arrested at London's The Cadogan Hotel (now The Belmond Cadogan Hotel), Rudyard Kipling wrote The Jungle Book at Brown's Hotel, and Ian Fleming supposedly came up with the line "shaken, not stirred" at the Dukes Hotel bar.

THE BERKELEY

Address:
Wilton Place,
Knightsbridge, SW1X 7RL
Phone:
020 7235 6000
Website:
the-berkeley.co.uk

One of the swankiest hotels in London, known for its mix of contemporary and classic rooms, minimalist décor in the lobby, and fashionable clientele, The Berkeley is on every top traveler's hot list. It also contains a wing of Japanese-style rooms for those who love Asian decor. Situated in Knightsbridge, its proximity not only to Harvey Nichols and Harrods department stores but also the luxury boutiques in the surrounding area make it the perfect outpost for a day of shopping. The ever stylish Blue Bar and Marcus Wareing's restaurant create a perfect end to a long day in a city that provides an unlimited itinerary, and the fashion-inspired afternoon tea is not only one of the most decadent in the city, but by far the most exciting. Also nearby is Hyde Park, which provides countless activities for active families. During the summer, children and adults alike will love the hotel's chic rooftop pool, one of few in London, which in the winter includes a cinema with fires and hot chocolate.

THE CONNAUGHT

Address:
Carlos Place,
Mayfair, W1K 2AL
Phone:
020 7499 7070
Website:
the-connaught.co.uk

One of the most renowned hotels in the world and a top choice for celebrities, businessmen, and socialites, The Connaught is the ultimate classic luxury hotel. Located in Mayfair, a prime spot in London for high-end shopping and dining, the hotel boasts an undisputed reputation for its glamorous décor, impeccable service, and posh restaurants and bars, including one by acclaimed chef Hélène Darroze and another by Jean-Georges Vongerichten. The large, individually decorated rooms make it feel like a home away from home, and with beautiful, spacious suites, travelers will want to stay forever. The lower level is home to the tranquil, zen-like Aman Spa from Aman Resorts, an award-winning facility with dozens of treatments. For the younger set, there is an indoor pool with kid-friendly hours, treats on arrival, activity books, children's menus, and the list goes on. Holidays are a particularly special time, with such activities as Santa passing out gifts and horse-drawn carriage rides through Mayfair.

THE
CONNAUGHT HOTEL

THE FOUR SEASONS HOTEL LONDON AT PARK LANE

Address:
Hamilton Place, Park Lane,
Mayfair, W1J 7DR
Phone:
020 7499 0888
Website:
fourseasons.com

For those guests who love a very modern hotel, the Four Seasons at Park Lane is a popular choice. It is at the top of the list for many travelers because of its location on Hyde Park, its contemporary rooms and public spaces, and the spa on the top floor. It is also known for its children's amenities, which include personalized itineraries, activities, babyproofing services, toiletries, video games, babysitting services, and the list goes on. They even have special rates on adjoining rooms. Be sure to visit the highly acclaimed concierge to help with tickets to musicals, horseback riding in Hyde Park, and restaurant reservations.

THE GORING

Address:
15 Beeston Place,
Westminster, SW1W 0JW
Phone:
020 7396 9000
Website:
thegoring.com

The Goring might be the most quintessentially English hotel in London, helped by the fact that it is the only family-run hotel left in the city. Managed by the Goring family since 1910, it has always been known for its impeccable service and traditional country house–like accommodations, but was made even more famous in 2011 when the Duchess of Cambridge chose to get ready for her wedding to Prince William in one of the luxurious suites. It has been said that the queen is a fan of the hotel, often stopping by for tea, but the fact that it is also right around the corner from Westminster Abbey and Buckingham Palace made it a good choice for the wedding, and also a great choice for tourists with families hoping to walk to most of the sights in the city. The Goring is also renowned for its hospitality toward children, welcoming babies with baskets full of toys and other essentials, welcoming small children with activity packs and stuffed animals, and featuring a Bedtime Story Library full of books for all ages. They also provide opportunities to bake cakes and cookies with the resident chef while parents unwind in the bar or beautiful garden. Never will you feel more at home or more welcomed.

THE GORING HOTEL
The Goring
Forbes

THE HAYMARKET HOTEL

Address:
1 Suffolk Place,
West End, SW1Y 4HX
Phone:
020 7470 4000
Website:
firmdalehotels.com

If seeing the London sights is high on your list, The Haymarket Hotel is in the perfect location just off Trafalgar Square. It is within walking distance to the National Gallery, Big Ben, Westminster Abbey, and Buckingham Palace, and is also near the theater district, where adults and kids can see popular shows and musicals. The hotel itself is beautifully decorated, and like Number Sixteen on this list, is part of the Firmdale group owned and designed by renowned English decorator Kit Kemp. The rooms and suites are done in a cheerful, modern British style of bright colors and florals. There is even a gorgeous townhouse available with separate entrance, two bedrooms, kitchen, and dining area that is ideal for those families staying for longer periods of time. The hotel also features the well-known Brumus Bar and Restaurant, an indoor swimming pool, gym, and spa, and welcomes children with many special amenities.

A GLIMPSE

Each year, London buses travel around 302 million miles. That's over 12,000 times the circumference of the earth.

THE LANESBOROUGH

Address:
Hyde Park Corner,
Knightsbridge, SW1X 7TA
Phone:
020 7259 5599
Website:
oetkercollection.com/hotels/
the-lanesborough

Quite possibly the most formal of all the hotels on this list, The Lanesborough is renowned not only for its gorgeous stone façade, but also for its impeccable service and amenities. Located directly across from Hyde Park, guests enjoy large traditionally decorated rooms with unparalleled views, and following an extensive renovation in 2014, the furnishings are now even more beautiful. Guests can also enjoy personal butlers, a spa and fitness center, highly acclaimed concierge services, and elegant dining areas and bars, including Céleste restaurant, which has earned a Michelin star. While the hotel is more on the proper side, guests should not be dissuaded from staying with children. The Lanesborough provides many amenities for the younger set, such as mini-bathrobes, movies, games, special itineraries, and picnic baskets.

THE LANESBOROUGH

06.

SHOPPING + SPECIALTY FOR KIDS

ACCESSORIZE

Address: 443 The Strand,
Covent Garden, WC2R 0QU
Phone: 020 7240 7054
Website: uk.accessorize.com

Teen and pre-teen girls love this inexpensive chain store full of accessories. There are many locations, and we tend to stock up at Heathrow, but the one near Covent Garden is a great option.

AMAIA KIDS

Address: 14 Cale Street,
Chelsea, SW3 3QU
Phone: 020 7590 0999
Website: amaiakids.co.uk

Our fashionable London friends love this children's and baby boutique for classic clothing.

AMAIA KIDS

BENJAMIN POLLOCK'S TOY SHOP

Address: 44, The Market Building, Covent Garden, WC2E 8RF
Phone: 020 7379 7866
Website: pollocks-coventgarden.co.uk

Located in the Covent Garden market and founded in the 1880s, this shop features theatrical toys, including old-fashioned pop-up theaters.

BLUE ALMONDS BOUTIQUE

Address: 164 Walton Street,
Knightsbridge, SW3 2JL
Phone: 020 7584 8038
Website: bluealmonds.co.uk

Luxury children's cashmere, clothing, and furniture, and our personal go-to for baby gifts. The Duchess of Cambridge is a fan.

BONPOINT

Address: 197 Westbourne Grove,
Notting Hill, W11 2SB
Phone: 020 7792 2515

Address: 15 Sloane Street,
Knightsbridge, SW1X 9NB
Phone: 020 7235 1441

Address: 52–54 Marylebone High Street,
Marylebone, W1U 5HR
Phone: 020 7487 2512
Website: bonpoint.com

Adorable French clothing that is famously pricey but totally worth it.

BLUE ALMONDS BOUTIQUE

CARAMEL BABY AND CHILD

Address: 291 Brompton Road,
South Kensington, SW3 2DY
Phone: 020 7589 7001

Address: 77 Ledbury Road,
Notting Hill, W11 2AG
Phone: 020 7727 0906

Address: 38B Ledbury Rd,
Notting Hill, W11 2AB
Phone: 020 7792 4208
Website: caramel-shop.co.uk

Luxury British children's clothing and home goods.

HAMLEYS

Address: 188–196 Regent Street,
Central London, W1B 5BT
Phone: 371 704 1977
Website: hamleys.com

The famous toy mecca on Regent Street, open since 1881.

HARROD'S ICE CREAM PARLOUR

Address: 87–135 Brompton Road,
Knightsbridge, SW1X 7XL
Phone: 020 7893 8959
Website: harrods.com

Enjoy a variety of ice cream flavors, shakes, and desserts, then head upstairs to the designer children's section.

"

. . .TO TRAVEL

IS TO LIVE.

Hans Christian Andersen

HARRY POTTER SHOP AT PLATFORM 9 3/4

Address: Pancras Road,
Kings Cross, N1 9AP
Phone: 020 3196 7375
Website: harrypotterplatform934.com

Harry Potter enthusiasts will love this souvenir shop at Kings Cross station. There's even a place to take a photo next to the Platform 9 3/4 sign.

HUMMINGBIRD BAKERY

Address: 133 Portobello Road,
Notting Hill, W11 2DY

Address: 47 Old Brompton Road,
South Kensington, SW7 3JP

Address: 155A Wardour Street,
Soho, W1F 8WG

Phone: 020 7851 1795
Website: hummingbirdbakery.com

Highly considered the most popular cupcakes in London.

MARIE-CHANTAL

Address: 4 Motcomb Street,
Belgravia, SW1X 8JU
Phone: 020 7235 2757
Website: mariechantal.co.uk

Gorgeous children's clothing and accessories by the Princess of Greece.

MOTCOMB STREET

A GLIMPSE

Motcomb Street is full of great shopping, including the Marie-Chantal boutique.

RACHEL RILEY

Address: 82 Marylebone High Street,
Marylebone, W1U 4QW
Phone: 020 7935 8345
Website: rachelriley.co.uk

"The British luxury brand for children" could not be cuter, and the designer could not be nicer.

SEMMALINA

Address: 225 Ebury Street,
Belgravia, SW1W 8UT
Phone: 020 7730 9333
Website: semmalinastarbags.com

A variety of well-known clothing brands and toys in a cute space.

SEMMALINA

07.

SHOPPING + SPECIALTY FOR ADULTS

ASSOULINE

Address: 196A Piccadilly,
St. James's, W1J 9EY
Phone: 020 3034 3090
Website: assouline.com

The famous boutique specializes in coffee table books.

BAMFORD

Address: 104 Draycott Avenue,
Knightsbridge, SW3 3AE
Phone: 020 7259 4980

Address: 62 South Audley Street,
Mayfair, W1K 2QR
Phone: 020 7499 7994
Website: bamford.com

Beautiful, neutral clothing and cashmere, bath product's, and children's gifts by Lady Bamford. The Draycott Avenue location serves as a wellness spa.

BOND STREET

In the Mayfair neighborhood

The most upscale designer shopping street in London.

BAMFORD

BURLINGTON ARCADE

Address: 51 Piccadilly,
Mayfair, W1J 0QJ
Website: burlingtonarcade.com

This covered pedestrian street is full of the most beautiful little shops in London. In the 1800s when this was established, arcades were the equivalent to modern-day malls.

CHRISTIAN DIOR

Address: 160–162 New Bond Street,
Mayfair, W1S 2UE
Phone: 020 7355 5930
Website: dior.com

There are not many London stores more beautiful than this one.

BURLINGTON ARCADE

COVENT GARDEN

Close to Trafalgar Square in central London

Quirky boutiques, bookstores, and cafés on cobblestone streets.

DAUNT BOOKS MARYLEBONE

Address: 83–84 Marylebone High Street, Marylebone, W1U 4QW
Phone: 020 7224 2295
Website: dauntbooks.co.uk

Originally selling travel books–so of course we love it–this location of the popular chain store now has all genres and is known for its beautiful skylights.

DAYLESFORD ORGANIC

Address: 208–212 Westbourne Grove, Notting Hill, W11 2RH
Phone: 020 7313 8050
Website: daylesford.com

Organic food, hampers, and home goods, plus a great variety of gourmet baby meals. If you make it to the Cotswolds, be sure to visit the original outpost.

DEBONNAIRE

Phone: 020 7590 9350
Website: debonnaire.com

This highly curated shop is a must for unique gifts. By appointment only.

"

WHY, SIR, YOU FIND NO MAN,

AT ALL INTELLECTUAL, WHO IS

WILLING TO LEAVE LONDON.

NO, SIR, WHEN A MAN IS

TIRED OF LONDON, HE IS TIRED

OF LIFE; FOR THERE IS IN LONDON

ALL THAT LIFE CAN AFFORD.

Samuel Johnson

DOVER STREET MARKET

Address: 18–22 Haymarket,
West End, SW1Y 4DG
Phone: 020 7518 0680
Website: london.doverstreetmarket.com

Gorgeous designer clothing in a chic, warehouse-like space.

ERDEM

Address: 70 South Audley Street,
Mayfair, W1K 2RA
Phone: 020 3653 0360
Website: erdem.com

This quintessentially English designer brand houses the most beautiful floral-printed clothing in a gorgeous building in Mayfair.

FOUND AND VISION

Address: 318 Portobello Road,
Notting Hill, W10 5RU
Phone: 020 8964 5656
Website: foundandvision.com

This vintage designer clothing store near Portobello Road is all the rage with the stylish set.

ERDEM

HARRODS

Address: 87–135 Brompton Road,
Knightsbridge, SW1X 7XL
Phone: 020 7730 1234
Website: harrods.com

There's nothing like the Harrods food hall or luxury children's clothing and toy departments.

HARVEY NICHOLS

Address: 109–125 Knightsbridge,
Knightsbridge, SW1X 7RJ
Phone: 020 7235 5000
Website: harveynichols.com

A popular designer department store very close to Harrods but without the tourists.

HATCHARDS

Address: 187 Piccadilly,
St. James's, W1J 9LE
Phone: 020 7439 9921
Website: hatchards.co.uk

The oldest bookshop in London.

A GLIMPSE

The 1986 London fashion week saw both the then-prime minister, Margaret Thatcher, and Diana, Princess of Wales, in attendance.

HEYWOOD HILL

Address: 10 Curzon Street,
Mayfair, W1J 5HH
Phone: 020 7629 0647
Website: heywoodhill.com

Another beloved bookstore selling old, new, and rare.

HOLLAND AND HOLLAND

Address: 33 Bruton Street,
Mayfair, W1J 6HH
Phone: 020 7499 4411
Website: hollandandholland.com

Luxury hunting and shooting attire with gun room, open since 1835.

HEYWOOD HILL

ILAPOTHECARY STORE AND TREATMENT ROOM

Address: 99 Kensington Church Street, Kensington, W8 7LN
Phone: 020 7342 168 395
Website: ilapothecary.com

A popular health and wellness shop.

JOHN LOBB

Address: 9 Saint James Street,
West End, SW1A 1EF
Phone: 020 7930 3664
Website: johnlobbltd.co.uk

Royals shop here for custom-made shoes.

LIBERTY

Address: Regent Street,
Soho, W1B 5AH
Phone: 020 3893 3062
Website: liberty.co.uk

Our go-to for amazing gifts and high-end designers; the origin of the "Liberty print."

MCQUEENS

Address: 29 North Audley Street,
Mayfair, W1K 6WY
Phone: 020 7251 5505
Website: mcqueens.co.uk

London's renowned florist.

MELROSE AND MORGAN

Address: 42 Gloucester Avenue,
Primrose Hill, NW1 8JD
Phone: 020 7722 0011
Website: melroseandmorgan.com

Various food items beautifully packaged; located just north of the London zoo.

LIBERTY

MOUNT STREET

In Mayfair

More top designer boutiques, like Goyard.

NINA CAMPBELL

Address: 9 Walton Street,
Chelsea, SW3 2JD
Phone: 020 7225 1011
Website: shop.ninacampbell.com

We love popping into this charming interior design shop for pretty gifts.

OTTOLENGHI

Address: 63 Ledbury Road,
Notting Hill, W11 2AD
Phone: 020 7727 1121

Address: 13 Motcomb Street,
Belgravia, SW1X 8LB
Phone: 020 7823 2707
Website: ottolenghi.co.uk

Well-known Mediterranean take-away deli with hampers and gourmet pantry items.

NINA CAMPBELL

PHILIP TREACY

Address: 69 Elizabeth Street,
Belgravia, SW1 W9PJ
Phone: 020 7730 3992
Website: philiptreacy.co.uk

London's most famous milliner, who has created hats for every royal wedding and society event.

PIPPA SMALL

Address: 201 Westbourne Grove,
Notting Hill, W11 2SB
Phone: 020 7792 1292
Website: pippasmall.com

The Duchess of Cambridge is a fan of the ethically made fine jewelry designs, and so are we.

PORTOBELLO ROAD

Address: Portobello Road,
Notting Hill, W11 2DY
Phone: 020 7361 3001
Website: portobelloroad.co.uk

Eccentric finds at this famous, old street market.

RALPH LAUREN

Address: 1 New Bond Street,
Mayfair, W1S 3RL
Phone: 020 7535 4600
Website: ralphlauren.co.uk

There is nothing more beautiful than a Ralph Lauren store, or the clothes he designs.

"

THERE'S NOWHERE ELSE

LIKE LONDON. NOTHING AT

ALL, ANYWHERE.

Vivienne Westwood

ROCOCO CHOCOLATES

Address: 5 Motcomb Street,
Belgravia, SW1X 8JU
Phone: 020 7245 0993
Website: rococochocolates.com

A beautiful, sophisticated chocolate shop and one of our favorite places to stock up on gifts for loved ones.

SELFRIDGES

Address: 400 Oxford Street,
Mayfair, W1A 1AB
Phone: 0800 123400
Website: selfridges.com

Local London it-girls know to shop at Selfridges department store.

SWAINE ADENEY BRIGG & HERBERT JOHNSON

Address: 7 Piccadilly Arcade,
Jermyn Street, St. James's,
SW1Y 6NH
Phone: 020 7409 7277
Website: swaineadeneybrigg.com

THE umbrella shop in London, along with Herbert Johnson hats, luggage, and other travel goods.

SELFRIDGES

THE BERKELEY TEA

Address: Wilton Place,
Knightsbridge, SW1X 7RL
Phone: 020 7107 8866
Website: the-berkeley.co.uk

Ladies and teenage girls will love this tea because the pastries and dishes are based on the season's designer fashions.

THE LADBROKE ARMS

Address: 54 Ladbroke Road,
Notting Hill, W11 3NW
Phone: 020 7727 6648
Website: ladbrokearms.com

This charming gastropub is frequented
by many interesting locals.

THE RITZ TEA

Address: 150 Piccadilly,
St. James's, W1J 9BR
Phone: 020 7300 2345
Website: theritzlondon.com

This gorgeous hotel in London has an elegant
afternoon tea that is also great for families.

THE SURPRISE

Address: 6 Christchurch Terrace,
Chelsea, SW3 4AJ
Phone: 020 7351 6954
Website: thesurprisechelsea.co.uk

This pub is frequented by residents of
London's chic Chelsea neighborhood.

TROY LONDON

Website: troylondon.com

Before a trip, be sure to shop TROY
London for stylish, English attire.

THE RITZ TEA

08.

EXPERIENCES FOR THE WHOLE FAMILY

APSLEY HOUSE

Address: 149 Piccadilly,
Hyde Park Corner, W1J 7NT
Phone: 020 7499 5676
Website: wellingtoncollection.co.uk

The mansion of the Dukes of Wellington can be found on Hyde Park Corner and is one of our favorite museum visits with older kids. The interiors and art collection are stunning, and if you time it right, you can get great photos of the Queen's Guard riding their horses to and from the Hyde Park stables.

BIG BUS TOURS

Website: bigbustours.com

Our secret to combating jet lag with kids in tow is to take a bus tour upon landing from an overseas flight–that way, they can take a nap. We also love the seasonal Night Tour for gorgeous sunset views of London's famous monuments.

BRITISH MUSEUM

Address: Great Russell Street,
Bloomsbury, WC1B 3DG
Phone: 020 7323 8299
Website: britishmuseum.org

This beautiful museum holds a collection of the world's greatest art and artifacts.

APSLEY HOUSE

BUCKINGHAM PALACE

Website: royalcollection.org.uk

The world's most famous palace gives tours from July through early September, but be sure to check the website for exact dates. Children will love the Family Pavilion with activities and games, and don't forget to tour the Royal Mews to see the family's historic carriages and cars.

BUCKINGHAM PALACE CHANGING OF THE GUARD

Address: Buckingham Palace, Westminster, SW1A 1AA
Website: changing-guard.com

From April to July, enjoy watching the guards ceremoniously change rifles and horses, everyday at 11:30, although the music begins at 11:15 a.m. The rest of the year it is every other day, so be sure to check the schedule.

CHELSEA PHYSIC GARDEN

Address: 66 Royal Hospital Road, Chelsea, SW3 4HS
Phone: 020 7352 5646
Website: chelseaphysicgarden.co.uk

Originally established in the 1600s as a place to grow plants for medicine, it is now a gorgeous botanical garden with café and shop.

BUCKINGHAM PALACE

CHURCHILL WAR ROOMS

Address: Clive Steps,
King Charles Street, SW1A 2AQ
Phone: 020 7416 5000
Website: iwm.org.uk

A personal favorite, adults and older kids will love learning about Winston Churchill and seeing the underground War Rooms where he commanded during WWII.

CLARENCE HOUSE

Address: Clarence House, St James's Palace, London, SW1A 1BA
Website: rct.uk/visit/clarence-house

The royal household of The Prince of Wales and the Duchess of Cornwall is open to the public during the summer months. Check the website for times and tickets.

CUTTY SARK

Address: King William Walk, Greenwich, SE10 9HT
Phone: 020 8858 4422
Website: rmg.co.uk/cutty-sark

This 1800s ship is so fun for kids to explore.

FROGMORE HOUSE

Address: Frogmore House, Windsor Home Park, Windsor, Berkshire, SL4
Website: rct.uk/visit/frogmore-house

This royal house and gardens, purchased by Queen Charlotte in 1790, are open three days during the year in August. Check the website for details.

“

LONDON

IS ON THE

WHOLE THE MOST

POSSIBLE FORM

OF LIFE.

Henry James

GO APE BATTERSEA PARK

Address: Battersea Park,
Battersea, SW11 4NJ
Phone: 020 1603 895 500
Website: goape.co.uk

Just across the river from Chelsea is a treetop adventure park full of zip lines and ropes courses. There are also adventure playgrounds, pedal boating, and a zoo nearby.

HYDE PARK

London's equivalent to Central Park has jogging trails, horseback riding, the Princess Diana playground, Kensington Palace, the Serpentine Gallery, and much more.

KENSINGTON PALACE

Address: Kensington Gardens,
Kensington, W8 4PX
Phone: 020 3166 6000
Website: hrp.org.uk/kensington-palace

Princess Diana's former residence, and currently the home of the Duke and Duchess of Cambridge, is located in Hyde Park and has a great museum to tour.

LEGOLAND

Address: Winkerfield Road,
Windsor, Berkshire, SL4 4AY
Phone: 1 844 740 9223
Website: legoland.co.uk

This popular theme park is just a short train ride from London.

LONDON AQUARIUM

Address: Sea Life London Aquarium,
County Hall, Westminster Bridge Road,
SE1 7PB
Phone: 020 371 663 1679
Website: visitsealife.com/london

More than 300 species to see, plus daily events including tank dives, talks, and feeding times.

LONDON DUNGEON

Address: Riverside Building, County Hall,
Westminster Bridge Road, SE1 7PB
Phone: 020 7654 0809
Website: thedungeons.com/london/en

Theatrical shows, stories, and rides based on London's historic dark side. Very entertaining for ages 8 and older.

LONDON EYE

Address: County Hall,
Westminster Bridge Road, SE1 7PB
Phone: 020 870 990 8881
Website: londoneye.com

Kids will love this enclosed glass Ferris wheel. Swarmed by tourists, but many think worth it for the views of London.

LONDON TRANSPORTATION MUSEUM

Address: Covent Garden Piazza,
Covent Garden, WC2E 7BB
Phone: 020 343 222 5000
Website: ltmuseum.co.uk

Our young kids absolutely love this museum full of buses, trains, and vehicles that you can climb on. It's also fun to walk around Covent Garden afterwards.

LONDON ZOO

Address: Regents Park, NW1 4RY
Phone: 020 7722 3333
Website: zsl.org/zsl-london-zoo

With thousands of animals and species plus a petting area and butterfly house, kids will be entertained for hours.

A GLIMPSE

The London Zoo was home to one of the most famous animals in the world: Winnie-the-Pooh.

Winnie was a female black bear, given to the zoo by the Canadian regiment that was called up to fight in France during the First World War. During Winnie's time at the London zoo, from 1915 until her death in 1934, she was much loved for her playfulness and gentleness.

Among her fans was author A.A. Milne and his son, Christopher Robin, who consequently changed the name of his own teddy bear to "Winnie-the-Pooh," providing the inspiration for his father's stories about Winnie-the-Pooh.

NATIONAL GALLERY

Address: Trafalgar Square,
Charing Cross, WC2N 5DN
Phone: 020 7747 2885
Website: nationalgallery.org.uk

One of London's most famous art museums, featuring works by da Vinci, Turner, and Van Gogh. Our kids love to see the enormous lion statues out front.

NATURAL HISTORY MUSEUM

Address: Cromwell Road,
South Kensington, SW7 5BD
Phone: 020 7942 5000
Website: nhm.ac.uk

View dinosaur fossils, build a volcano, visit the wildlife garden, and learn all about the earth and evolution.

NATIONAL PORTRAIT GALLERY

Address: St. Martin's Place,
Charing Cross, WC2H 0HE
Phone: 020 7306 0055
Website: npg.org.uk

Here you can view paintings and photographs of historical British figures.

NATIONAL GALLERY AND TRAFALGAR SQUARE

PRINCESS DIANA MEMORIAL PLAYGROUND

Address: Kensington Gardens, The Broad Walk, W2 2UH
Website: royalparks.org.uk/parks/kensington-gardens

The ultimate playground, with a giant pirate ship, teepees, toys, and play sculptures.

ROYAL BOTANIC GARDENS, KEW

Address: Richmond, TW9 3AB
Phone: 020 8332 5655
Website: kew.org

Gorgeous gardens and a treetop walkway, plus special areas and activities for young children.

ROYAL OPERA HOUSE

Address: Bow Street,
Covent Garden, WC2E 9DD
Phone: 020 7240 1200
Website: roh.org.uk

We love seeing *The Nutcracker* ballet here over the holidays, and there are many other wonderful performances throughout the year.

SCIENCE MUSEUM WONDERLAB

Address: Exhibition Road,
South Kensington, SW7 2DD
Phone: 020 333 241 4000
Website: sciencemuseum.org.uk

Kids will love this interactive gallery at the Science Museum, where they can learn about all kinds of science-related topics through hands-on experiences.

SHAKESPEARE'S GLOBE THEATER

Address: 21 New Globe Walk,
Bankside, SE1 9DT
Phone: 020 7401 9919
Website: shakespearesglobe.com

For grownups or the family with teenagers studying Shakespeare in high school, this theater demonstrates what an actual play was like during the 1600s.

SIR JOHN SOANES MUSEUM

Address: 13 Lincoln's Inn Fields,
Holborn, WC2A 3BP
Phone: 020 7405 2107
Website: soane.org

This gorgeous old townhouse is now a museum full of paintings and antiquities gathered by architect John Soane.
Best for adults and older kids.

“

THE PARKS BE

THE LUNGS OF

LONDON.

Charles Dickens

SOMERSET HOUSE

Address: Strand, WC2R 1LA
Phone: 020 7845 4600
Website: somersethouse.org.uk

There are so many exhibits and cultural events to see at Somerset House, and it is particularly fun in the winter when the courtyard turns into a skating rink. We also love Spring, the museum's gorgeous restaurant, and the Fortnum & Mason pop-up in the winter.

TATE MODERN

Address: Bankside, SE1 9TG
Phone: 020 7887 8888
Website: tate.org.uk

There is always an amazing art exhibit to be seen at this world-renowned museum. Afterward, it is fun to walk over the River Thames on the Millenium Bridge.

THE PALACE OF WESTMINSTER

Address: SW1A 0AA
Phone: 020 7219 3000
Website: parliament.uk

More commonly known as Parliament, visitors can tour this beautiful, historic building, or attend hearings and debates. Check the website to book tickets.

SOMERSET HOUSE

THE SHERLOCK HOLMES MUSEUM

Address: 221B Baker Street,
Marylebone, NW1 6XE
Phone: 020 7224 3688
Website: sherlock-holmes.co.uk

This museum is dedicated to the literary figure, and it's fun to see what a Victorian-era home looked like.

TOWER OF LONDON

Address: London, EC3N 4AB
Phone: 020 3166 6000
Website: hrp.org.uk/toweroflondon/

View the crown jewels, tour an ancient fortress, make your own helmet, and play games. Better for older children as not every area is stroller accessible, and some exhibits and tours can seem frightening to small kids.

VICTORIA AND ALBERT MUSEUM

Address: Cromwell Road, Knightsbridge, SW7 2RL
Phone: 020 7942 2000
Website: vam.ac.uk

While more suited for adults, this museum holds the most interesting cultural exhibitions, and every now and then one that kids will enjoy, so be sure to check out what's on. The museum's shop is a great place to find gifts.

VICTORIA AND ALBERT MUSEUM OF CHILDHOOD

Address: Cambridge Heath Road, Bethnal Green, E2 9PA
Phone 020 8983 5200
Website: vam.ac.uk/moc

This branch of the museum specializes in objects for children.

TOWER OF LONDON

WARNER BROTHERS STUDIO TOUR: THE MAKING OF HARRY POTTER

Address: Studio Tour Drive,
Leavesden, WD25 7LR
Phone: 44 345 084 0900
Website: wbstudiotour.co.uk

A behind-the-scenes tour of the movie set. Kids will also love riding the train from London to the studio.

WESTMINSTER ABBEY

Address: 20 Deans Yard, SW1P 3PA
Phone: 020 7222 5152
Website: westminster-abbey.org

This royal church is a World Heritage Site founded in 960 AD. Book tickets in advance because lines can be very long.

WEST END SHOWS

Website: londontheatre.co.uk

The equivalent to Broadway in New York, the West End brings the world's best shows to the stage.

WESTMINSTER ABBEY

WINDSOR CASTLE

Website: rct.uk/visit/windsor-castle

Most recently in the news as the wedding venue of the Duke and Duchess of Sussex, this is the oldest and largest castle residence in the world, vacated on many weekends throughout the year by the queen of England. It is open to the public, but check the website for opening times.

09.

SEASONAL EVENTS

CHELSEA FLOWER SHOW

Every May, the Royal Horticultural Society hosts a huge flower show at the Royal Hospital Chelsea, and local storefronts and restaurants also take part with gorgeous flower displays.
Website: rhs.org.uk

HYDE PARK WINTER WONDERLAND

The whole family will love the rides, vendors, and food stands in Hyde Park during the holidays.
Website:
hydeparkwinterwonderland.com

LONDON FASHION WEEK

September and February bring about the country's biggest fashion designers to display their creations on runways at Somerset House and elsewhere throughout the city. Mere mortals can register to attempt to score tickets.
Website: britishfashioncouncil.co.uk

LONDON HOLIDAY SEASON

London is magical in December and January, with festive lights, markets, ice-skating, caroling concerts, New Year's Eve fireworks along the River Thames, a New Year's Day parade in central London, and much more.
Website:
timeout.com/london/christmas

MASTERPIECE

Art and design enthusiasts unite for an exhibition in late June that brings together the world's most desired art, jewelery, and furniture collectors.
Website: masterpiecefair.com

ROYAL ASCOT

The year's most popular horse race includes a procession by the royal family alongside Michelin-starred meals and designer clothing and millinery worn by racegoers.
Website: ascot.co.uk

THE BOAT RACE

The most important boat race of the year takes place in early April, as spectators watch Oxford and Cambridge University students compete along the Thames.
Website: theboatrace.org

THE PROMS

The world's most famous conductors and orchestras descend upon the Royal Albert Hall for several weeks of concerts beginning in July.
Website:
royalalberthall.com/tickets/proms

TROOPING THE COLOUR

The entire royal family comes out to celebrate the Queen's official birthday in June with a Horse Guard's Parade and Royal Air Force plane salute.
Website: royal.uk/trooping-colour

WIMBLEDON

Take the older kids to a tennis match at one of the most famous tournaments in the world. Last minute tickets can be acquired at the venue early in the morning, or tour the site's museum when the tournament is not in session.
Website: wimbledon.com

THE ERDEM SHOW DURING
LONDON FASHION WEEK

10.

SAMPLE ITINERARIES

These sample itineraries are appropriate for all ages. We have kept them light because we all know kids' moods can be unpredictable. For more age-specific activities, please go through our Experiences for the Whole Family section, which also gives more details on each recommendation listed in this section.

DAY ONE

MORNING

After breakfast at your hotel, which we find much easier to manage when traveling with kids who have woken up hungry (hotel breakfasts are also free if you book with Glimpse), head to the northwest corner of **Hyde Park** to enjoy the **Princess Diana Memorial Playground**.

Next, begin walking south and, on the way, you can admire **Kensington Palace,** where many royals live and work, although we do not recommend touring with small kids.

LUNCH

Depending on how much time was spent at the playground, you can head to lunch at **Daphne's** or make a stop at **Harvey Nichols** for some shopping. Kids will also love the **Harrods** food hall for dessert.

AFTERNOON

Next, head down the road to the **Natural History Museum**. Plan to spend a few hours here.

DINNER

Finally, head to nearby **Harry's Dolce Vita** for an early dinner.

DAY TWO

MORNING

After breakfast, saunter around **Mayfair**, admiring the beautiful parks and architecture, as well as the high-end shops.

Right in between Mayfair and Piccadilly is **Hamley's** toy store, and just up the street, **Liberty**. Both are great English shopping institutions.

LUNCH

Head just south of Hamley's to **The Wolseley** to enjoy a chic lunch.

AFTERNOON

Hail a taxi outside The Wolseley and head to the **London Zoo** for a fun afternoon of animals and adventure. Afterward, choose any restaurant on our list for dinner.

A GLIMPSE

Every year since 1947, Norway has gifted the Trafalgar Square Christmas tree, thanking England for their alliance during WWII.

DAY THREE

MORNING

Spend the morning running around **St. James Park** or touring **Buckingham Palace** during the summer. Plan to be at the front gates at 11:15 a.m. for the changing of the guard.

LUNCH

Head to **The Ritz** and enjoy a quintessential afternoon tea for lunch. We find it to be filling enough for a whole meal.

AFTERNOON

Across the Thames, spend the afternoon on the **London Eye** and at the **Aquarium**. Afterward, head to **Covent Garden**.

DINNER

The Ivy Chelsea Garden is such a great lunch spot, but it's also good for an early dinner with the kids. The taxi ride from Covent Garden will take up a good chunk of time, while also providing a nice tour of the city.

“

THE BEST BRIBE WHICH
LONDON OFFERS TO-DAY TO THE
IMAGINATION, IS, THAT, IN SUCH
A VAST VARIETY OF PEOPLE AND
CONDITIONS, ONE CAN BELIEVE
THERE IS ROOM FOR PERSONS OF
ROMANTIC CHARACTER TO EXIST,
AND THAT THE POET, THE MYSTIC,
AND THE HERO MAY HOPE TO
CONFRONT THEIR COUNTERPARTS.

Ralph Waldo Emerson

If traveling without kids or just taking some time on your own (with the help of a nanny or hired sitter), we suggest the following itinerary.

DAY WITHOUT KIDS

MORNING

Start with a light breakfast at **Cecconi's**, followed by high-end shopping in **Mayfair**. We also love gallery-hopping in this neighborhood. Afterward, we love **Churchill War Rooms**, and that will take you near Big Ben, **Westminster Abbey,** and 10 Downing Street. A tour of the **British Museum** is also recommended.

LUNCH

Enjoy a leisurely meal with wine at **Dinings**.

AFTERNOON

From **Dinings,** walk to the **Victoria and Albert Museum** for one of their iconic exhibits.

DINNER

Book a table at **Gymkhana** for a long meal or go for a pre-theater bite at **The Ivy** if going to a show in the **West End**.

AFTER DINNER OR A SHOW

Drinks at **Chiltern Firehouse** or at **The Connaught** hotel are a must. Or go to both–absolutely no judgment.

BEWARE
HORSES MAY KICK
OR BITE!
THANK

11.

CITY TIPS + HELPFUL INFORMATION

GETTING AROUND

Buses are a great way to see London, and kids love the top floor of the double-deckers. Tickets can be purchased at machines close to each stop, where you'll also find bus routes and timetables.

If you will be in London at least a week and plan to use public transportation, it would be easier to purchase Oyster cards at newspaper stores. They are pre-paid, plastic cards that can be used on buses and the underground Tube.

If renting a car, be sure to confirm with the rental agency that you will be driving into London. Otherwise, you will receive a mailed ticket for congestion charges.

All hotels can set up chauffeured car services, either around town or to and from the airports. Alternatively, taxis can easily be hailed from the streets, and they line up at the airports. If you prefer not to make the drive into the city from the airports (Heathrow can take up to an hour while Gatwick can take 1½ hours), you can choose to ride the 15-minute Tube from Heathrow to Paddington Station, or take a half-hour train ride from Gatwick to Victoria Station. After clearing customs at the airports, follow signs to the train, or the Heathrow Express, and once you arrive at your destination at the stations, follow signs to the taxi queues.

A GLIMPSE

In London, if paying with cash, it is customary to exit the cab beforehand.

BABY FOOD, DIAPERS, ETC.

London is full of pharmacies and the most common is Boots. They also stock all baby paraphernalia.

For organic baby food, there is a Whole Foods in Piccadilly Circus on Glasshouse Street and in Kensington on Kensington High Street. Daylesford Organic also creates gourmet baby food.

BABYSITTING

Each hotel we have listed is able to find reputable babysitters, but most require at least 24-hours notice. Alternatively, Rockabye Sitters is London's premiere agency for families and upscale hotels. *Website:* rockabyesitters.co.uk

BATHROOMS

A few public restrooms are scattered throughout the city. Some areas include the Covent Garden square (only accessed by stairs), near Marlborough Gate, at the entrance to St. James's Park near Trafalgar Square, and opposite Westminster Abbey.

Alternatively, you can opt for a nearby café.

GIVE WAY

EMBASSIES

For a complete list with contact information by country go to gov.uk/government/publications/foreign-embassies-in-the-uk

HEALTH CARE

Children's hospital:
Great Ormond Street Hospital
Phone: 020 7405 9200

For other health-related issues, please contact your hotel concierge for direction.

LOST ITEMS

The website for London's public transportation lost property office is tfl.gov.uk

POLICE AND EMERGENCIES

Dial 999 for the police or ambulances in the event of an emergency.

For non-emergencies, dial 101 for the police.

A GLIMPSE

There is one street in London
where you have to drive on the wrong
side of the road: the entrance to
the Savoy Hotel.

The Savoy is said to require this
in order for taxis to drop off customers at
the Savoy Theatre, which is on the right-
hand side of the road, before picking
up guests at the hotel.

STROLLERS

Many museums and sites have stroller parking areas, although the employees cannot be held responsible in the event of theft. Depending on the size of the venue, it may be wiser to coat check them and let kids walk or be carried in a sling.

No need to break down strollers when getting into London's spacious taxis. Unless it is a double stroller, it will fit right through the door.

There is a section for up to two strollers on London buses, which is easier than getting on and off the underground Tube trains.

Journey Planner, a helpful trip-planning website, can show you which Tube routes and lines to take that will not involve any stairs. journeyplanner.tfl.gov.uk

Try to avoid public transportation during rush hour, which is 7 a.m. to 9 a.m., and 4 p.m. to 6:30 p.m.

TIPPING

At a restaurant, a 15% tip is customary, although some will automatically include a service charge, so be sure to look over the bill.

It is not common to tip in bars or pubs.

Taxi drivers usually receive an extra 10–15% of the fare.

Two pounds per bag is a normal tip for each porter at a hotel, as is one pound when they hail you a taxi upon exiting the hotel. At upscale hotels you may feel it appropriate to give more.

Always tip the concierge per reservation, ticket procurement, etc.

Some hotels will include a service charge on the bill. If not, be sure to leave something for housekeeping. Because all hotels listed in our guide are upscale, a daily tip is encouraged as the staff may differ from day to day.

3

12.

PACKING

When traveling, we recommend listing exact outfits for each day in order to avoid overpacking and to stay organized. We also encourage mixing and matching key pieces, so you have more room for purchases. We then place items either in packing cubes, or directly in the suitcase starting with the last day, so you are not digging for clothing packed for day one.

DAY ONE

Morning: ....

....

....

....

....

....

Evening: ....

....

....

....

....

....

Kids: ....

....

....

....

....

....

THE CONNAUGHT

DAY TWO

Morning: ....

....

....

....

....

....

Evening: ....

....

....

....

....

....

Kids: ....

....

....

....

....

....

DAY THREE

Morning: ....

....

....

....

....

....

Evening: ....

....

....

....

....

....

Kids: ....

....

....

....

....

....

DAY FOUR

Morning:

Evening:

Kids:

LONDON PACKING TIPS

Highlight or put a mark next to outfits once they're packed.

Layers are almost always essential in London.

DAY FIVE

Morning:

Evening:

Kids:

“

TRAVEL LIGHT, VERY LIGHT,

AND TAKE THINGS THAT CAN

WORK IN MANY WAYS. WHEN YOU

FIGURE OUT HOW TO PACK LIGHTLY,

YOU FIGURE OUT HOW TO

LIVE LIGHTLY.

Diane von Furstenberg

DAY SIX

Morning: ....

Evening: ....

Kids: ....

DAY SEVEN

Morning: ....

....

....

....

....

....

Evening: ....

....

....

....

....

....

Kids: ....

....

....

....

....

....

CARRY-ON

- ☐ Passport/ID
- ☐ Change of Clothes
  for yourself and the kids
- ☐ Bathing Suits
  in case you need to change your plans upon arrival, or in the case of lost luggage
- ☐ Laptop/Tablet
- ☐ Jewelry
- ☐ Camera
- ☐ Converter
- ☐ Headphones
- ☐ Chargers
- ☐ Glasses
- ☐ Medication and Supplements
- ☐ Books/Magazines
- ☐ Snacks
- ☐ Travel Wrap
- ☐ Coin Purse
  because coins are predominantly used in England
- ☐ Lotion
- ☐ Face Mist
- ☐ Lip Moisturizer

☐ Other: ....

....

....

....

....

KIDS

- [ ] Tablet/iPad
- [ ] Headphones
- [ ] Backpacks
- [ ] Coats/Jackets
- [ ] Snacks
- [ ] Toys
- [ ] Other: ....

....

....

....

BABIES

- [ ] Bottle and Formula/Milk
- [ ] Pacifier
- [ ] Snacks
- [ ] Blankets
- [ ] Toys
- [ ] Other: ....

....

....

EXTRAS

- [ ] Workout Clothes
- [ ] Coats/Jackets
- [ ] Lingerie
- [ ] Toiletries
- [ ] Other: ....

13.

TIPS FROM THE EXPERTS

HOW TO GET THE MOST OUT OF YOUR TRAVEL EXPERIENCES

BY MELINDA STEVENS, EDITOR-IN-CHIEF OF CONDÉ NAST TRAVELLER

1. Plan, but don't overplan! The best stuff happens in the places in-between–the surprises, the unexpected–being loose enough to go with the flow, so you can get happily caught up where the best experiences are unfolding, not with what the schedule dictates.

2. Travel, really, is mostly about the people. Meeting people in the place you have travelled to–having drinks with them, going to their houses, hearing about their lives–is what takes a standard trip and moves it onto a different level. Open your hearts and minds! Be alert to this possibility, even if you are normally a shy person. Find out where the locals dance, not the tourists, where they eat and hang out and shop. This will give you an infinitely better understanding of a place and a people who are different from you. Which is the point.

3. Take your time. Sure, it's fun to go somewhere for a quick jaunt. I went to Norway for 16 hours to see the White Lights, and I once seemingly went to Shanghai for a bath. But it's only by taking your time, stretching it out, being somewhere for any considered length at all that will unhook you from your normal schedule and allow you to be more expansive with your horizons, literally and metaphorically.

4. Reward good work. Choose to stay in places that have more than their own pockets in mind. How is your hotel connected to its community, how does it support it, is it known for its good works, in any variety of ways, from protecting biodiversity to adhering to sound sustainable practices?

5. Tread lightly. In all ways. You are a guest in other people's lands. Understand the rules, be aware and be curious, hold back on your brashness, pick up your rubbish, pay your way, be generous and thoughtful with your time and your money. Contribute and engage. Your tourists bucks are a powerful tool, use them in the right way. Be a good human making good decisions.

MELINDA'S LONDON FAVORITES

I like going east, to Dalston and Shoreditch, to the roadside cafés and Colombia Road flower market, to the Tate Modern for the drama as well as the art. But also west, where I live, to little special old-school pubs like the Anglesea in Shepherds Bush.

HOW TO STAY GROUNDED WHILE TRAVELING

BY WARIS AHLUWALIA, ACTOR, DESIGNER, AND FOUNDER OF HOUSE OF WARIS

1. Prepare. Mostly I think about food–traveling or not. However, planes get delayed, road trips take longer, etc. It's best to be prepared, so you're not forced to eat junk food that's readily available everywhere in the world. Pack snacks. Always. For me it's raw almonds, raw cashews, low-sugar protein bars.

2. Hydrate. Bring a water bottle. Buy water. Whatever the situation, drink water. Dehydration causes headaches, makes you feel tired, and can lead to loss of strength and stamina. You need strength and stamina every day but especially when you're traveling.

3. Get Outside. Find the sunshine or at the very least some fresh air. Go outside and feel the sun on your face. It can help reset your body clock. Skip the nap and adjust to your new time zone.

4. Exercise. Any movement helps me tremendously. Healthy body, healthy mind. Use the hotel gym, go for a run in the neighborhood, or find a local park. There's nothing more grounding than the earth, grass, and trees.

5. Breathe. Deeply. Not the way we normally do, with shallow breaths. But intentional, slow breathing. Deep breathing can immediately lower your heart rate and blood pressure.

WARIS'S LONDON FAVORITES

The Connaught hotel, Alex Eagle for shopping, Dishroom restaurant, The Wolseley for breakfast, and The Cow gastropub.

TIPS FROM THE LOCALS

BY ERDEM MORALIOGLU, FASHION DESIGNER

FAVORITE...

Hotel:
Claridges

Restaurant:
The River Café

Clothing Boutique:
ERDEM

Home Decor Boutique:
Sigmar

Bakery:
Violette

Specialty Shop:
Donlon Books

Museum:
National Portrait Gallery

Neighborhood:
Bloomsbury

Park:
Regents Park

Hidden gem:
St. Georges Garden, Bloomsbury

ERDEM FW20 SHOW AT THE NATIONAL PORTRAIT GALLERY

If you had one last day in London, what would you do? I would grab a coffee and head to the London Library to draw and do research. Then go west for a pasta lunch at The River Café (Panzotti di Zucca or the Taglierini). I would head back to my neighborhood in Bloomsbury and then spend the afternoon exploring all the used bookstores on Marchmont Street. Then I would go for martinis at Dukes . . . after to J Sheekeys for a quick lobster burger or tuna steak for dinner. And finally go the Royal Opera House to watch a ballet.

SHOPPING TIPS WHILE TRAVELING

BY ROOPAL PATEL, FASHION DIRECTOR OF SAKS FIFTH AVENUE

1. Get lost! I like exploring local spots to find new shops when I visit somewhere for the first time. It's good to get lost and take your time. I have found so many treasures shopping this way.

2. Support and buy local. There is nothing better than discovering a new designer, artist, home goods ware, etc. for the first time. I always like coming home from my travels with a little keepsake that's special that reminds me of my trip.

3. Taste the town. I love to cook, especially new recipes I come across on my travels. I always visit the local grocery and bring back a few local spices, flavors, etc.

ROOPAL'S LONDON FAVORITES

The Wolseley is one of my favorite restaurants in London. I love the mix of English tradition and art deco glam. It's always a stop on every visit to London.

HOW TO GIVE BACK WHILE TRAVELING

BY LAUREN BUSH LAUREN, FOUNDER OF *FEED*

1. Support businesses doing good. Stay at hotels and resorts that prioritize more eco-friendly practices and community give-back programs.

2. Volunteer in the city. Find a local charity or community program and lend a helping hand. It could be a soup kitchen or a beach clean-up. It's also a good way to meet some of the locals.

3. Be active. Walking, biking, or taking public transport is a great way to get to know a new place, and it is also more environmentally friendly.

4. Explore art and culture. Support museums and other cultural institutions while traveling. Many depend on tourists' revenue to operate.

5. Shop local. Seek out the mom and pop boutiques and restaurants. These are also the most interesting and charming in my opinion.

LAUREN'S LONDON FAVORITES

The Tate Modern and Nopi restaurant.

TIPS FROM THE LOCALS

BY HANNAH CECIL GURNEY, DIRECTOR OF DE GOURNAY

FAVORITE...

Hotel:
The Haymarket

Restaurant:
Isabel, Mayfair

Clothing Boutique:
ERDEM, South Audley Street

Home Decor Boutique:
The Conran Shop

Bakery:
Gails

Specialty Shop:
Edition 94, Fulham Road

Spa:
The Aman Spa at The Connaught

Pub:
The Builders Arms, Chelsea

Museum:
V&A

Neighborhood:
Chelsea

Park:
Battersea

Hidden gem:
Annabel's, Mayfair

If you had one last day in London, what would you do? Brunch in Portobello Market followed by a dog walk around the Serpentine, then a long dinner at River Café.

HANNAH CECIL GURNEY
WITH HER SISTER RACHEL
(FEATURED ON PAGE 210)

BEAUTY TIPS WHILE TRAVELING

BY GUCCI WESTMAN, MAKEUP ARTIST AND FOUNDER OF WESTMAN ATELIER

1. Travel light. Travel with an edited makeup bag–it should be clean, purposeful, and curated. Travel and fragrance atomizers actually inspired the packaging for my Westman Atelier products. I love how atomizers are small and portable but still beautiful and functional.

2. Hydrate often. I'm a big believer in hydrating the skin from the inside-out. For an extra pick me up, I'll add an electrolyte tablet from Nuun to my water. My carry-on is never without a hydrating bio-cellulose mask and a rich moisturizer.

3. Refresh yourself. If jet-lag is catching up to you, you can fake a wide-awake look. Start with a highlighter under your foundation for an ethereal finish. Apply foundation under your eyes, using a brush in an upward motion to lift up the corners of your eyes. Spot check any redness as well. Sweep bronzer horizontally over the areas of your face that naturally get sun–cheeks, temples, forehead and eyelids. Don't forget under your eyes too. Pop a little rosy flush onto your cheeks and lips, and finish with a coat of mascara on the lashes.

4. Reset your energy. If time allows, exercise and a quick lymphatic drainage massage do wonders for the body. If not, take a few moments in the morning to stretch and meditate–it will reset your energy and lift up your mood.

5. Be inspired. Beauty should always be fun! When deciding what to pack in your bag, be inspired by where you are going and what you are doing. Have fun and experiment!

GUCCI'S LONDON FAVORITES

Spring Restaurant and the Belmond Cadogan hotel.

TIPS FROM THE LOCALS

BY ROSIE VAN CUTSEM AND LUCIA RUCK KEENE, CO-FOUNDERS OF TROY LONDON

FAVORITE...

Hotel: The Rosewood Hotel, tucked away in Holborn, for a quiet stay, and equipped with an excellent cocktail bar.

Restaurant: Wiltons in Mayfair is a real treat if you enjoy the finest fish with the best of old school service.

Clothing Boutique: NBT at Showcase, 12 Regent Street, is great for discovering emerging designers.

Home Decor Boutique: Kelling Designs, 3 Langton Street in Chelsea, has beautiful jewel tone goodies for your home.

Bakery: Pearl and Groove for the most sinful looking but somehow gluten-free cakes and treats.

Specialty Shop: VV Rouleaux–a heavenly swirl of ribbons and habberdashery supplies.

Spa: The Bulgari Hotel is a little oasis of pampering calm in the middle of Knightsbridge.

Pub: The Cow, Westbourne Park Road, for a glass of wine and pint of prawns.

Museum: The RA holds some wonderful exhibitions and is a beautiful place to while away an afternoon.

Neighborhood: Portobello holds a special place in our hearts as a characterful London hub.

Park: Richmond Park, not least because of the fabulous Petersham Nurseries.

Hidden gem: The Savile Club is a beautifully historic private club in Mayfair, definitely worth a visit to see their elegant gilt ballroom and oak panelled bar.

If you had one last day in London, what would you do? Brunch at Grangers on Westbourne Grove, a stroll through one of London's beautful parks, a mosey round the National Gallery, tapas at Barrafina in Covent Garden, and a show in the West End. If we still had the energy it would then be on to cocktails at Milk & Honey in Soho or toe tap to some jazz at Ronnie Scotts.

HOW TO CAPTURE THE MOMENTS WHILE TRAVELING

BY CLAIBORNE SWANSON FRANK, PHOTOGRAPHER AND AUTHOR

1. Camera ready. Take photos on automatic setting or iPhone, so you don't miss moments.

2. Finishing touch. I love using an app called Camera Plus to crop, filter, and frame my photos. It's awesome and gives the photos a finished vibe.

3. Album goals. Set out to create an album at the start of the trip, so you stay focused and committed.

4. Snap, snap. You can never take too many photos.

5. Be present. Turn your phone off often and be present to the beauty around you. Take in the adventure and the precious moments you are living. You never get those back.

CLAIBORNE'S LONDON FAVORITES

Claridge's, and walks in Hyde Park.

TIPS FROM THE LOCALS

BY RACHEL CECIL GURNEY, DIRECTOR OF SALES AT DE GOURNAY

FAVORITE...

Hotel:
Blakes Hotel

Restaurant:
The River Café

Clothing Boutique:
ERDEM

Home Decor:
Lots Road Auction House

Bakery:
Baker & Spice, Denyer Street

Specialty Shop:
Pet Pavilion to indulge my new blue chow chow

Spa:
Lanesborough Spa

Pub:
The Scarsdale Tavern, Edwardes Square

Museum:
Leighton House, Kensington

Neighborhood:
Chelsea

Park:
Richmond

Hidden gem:
Butler & Wilson, Fulham Road

If you had one last day in London, what would you do? I'd rent a boat and go west down the Thames from Parliament, taking in the view, to a stop for a stroll and picnic in Kew Gardens. I'd then spend the afternooon looking at the treasures that Syon & Ham House have to offer, returning home for cocktails at Blakes followed by dinner at Daphne's, an Italian favourite of ours!

“

I’D SPEND

THE DAY

ON A BOAT

AND GO WEST

DOWN THE THAMES

FROM PARLIAMENT,

TAKING IN

THE VIEW. . .

Rachel Gurney

TIPS FOR TRAVELING WITH KIDS

BY LILY ALDRIDGE, MOM, MODEL, AND ENTREPRENEUR

1. Snacks, snacks, and more snacks! I make sure to have their favorite snacks handy.

2. Call the hotel ahead of time. See what they provide in order to minimize packing (i.e., cribs, monitors, extra refrigerator for milk, kids snacks, etc.).

3. Never rely on your phone or airport wifi! Download movies, TV shows, and educational apps before arriving at the airport.

4. Middle section, please! On a redeye, I try to book seats in the middle of the cabin, away from noise and light.

5. Go with the flow.

LILY'S LONDON FAVORITE

High Tea at The Savoy.

14.

NOTES

NOTES

NOTES

NOTES

NOTES

NOTES

NOTES

NOTES

NOTES

NOTES

NOTES

NOTES

NOTES

“ONCE YOU HAVE TRAVELED,

BUT IS PLAYED OUT OVER AND OVER

THE MIND CAN NEVER BREAK

THE VOYAGE NEVER ENDS,

AGAIN IN THE QUIETEST CHAMBERS.

OFF FROM THE JOURNEY."

Pat Conroy

PHOTOGRAPHY CREDITS

Page 5 | Photograph
Copyright © Clea Ramos

Page 21 | Photograph
Copyright © Daphne's

Page 23 | Photograph
Copyright © Dinings SW3

Page 27 | Photograph
Copyright © Granger & Co

Page 28 | Photograph
Copyright © Gymkhana

Page 31 | Photograph
Copyright © Hakkasan by
Antony Rettie

Page 33 | Photograph
Copyright © Hélène Darroze
by Maybourne Hotel Group

Page 35 | Photograph
Copyright © Isabel Mayfair

Page 37 | Photograph
Copyright © J Sheekey

Page 41 | Photograph
Copyright © La Petite Maison

Page 45 | Photograph
Copyright © Scott's

Page 47 | Photograph
Copyright © The Archduke
by Black & Blue Group

Page 49 | Photograph
Copyright © The Ivy

Page 50 | Photograph
Copyright © The Ivy
Chelsea Garden

Page 53 | Photograph
Copyright © The River Café

Page 54 | Photograph
Copyright © The Wolseley

Page 62 | Photograph
Copyright © Core by
Clare Smyth

Page 65 | Photograph
Copyright © Jamavar

Page 70 | Photograph
Copyright © Claridge's by
Maybourne Hotel Group

Page 73 | Photograph
Copyright © Number Sixteen
Firmdale Hotels by Simon
Brown

Page 75 | Photograph
Copyright © The Berkeley by
Maybourne Hotel Group

Page 77 | Photograph
Copyright © The Connaught
by Maybourne Hotel Group

Page 78 | Photograph
Copyright © The Four
Seasons Hotel London
At Park Lane

Page 81 | Photograph
Copyright © The Goring

Page 83 | Photograph
Copyright © The Haymarket
Hotel Firmdale Hotels by
Simon Brown

Page 85 | Photograph
Copyright © The Lanesborough Oetker Collection

Page 88 | Photograph
Copyright © Amaia Kids

Page 91 | Photograph
Copyright © Blue Almonds Boutique

Page 97 | Photograph
Copyright © Semmalina

Page 101 | Photograph
Copyright © Bamford

Page 109 | Photograph
Copyright © Harrods

Page 110 | Photograph
Copyright © Heywood Hill by Horst Friedrichs

Page 119 | Photograph
Copyright © Selfridges

Page 121 | Photograph
Copyright © The Ritz London

Page 125 | Photograph
Copyright © English Heritage

Page 127 | Photograph
Copyright © Royal Collection Trust / © Her Majesty Queen Elizabeth II 2020

Page 138 | Photograph
Copyright © The Royal Opera House

Page 143 | Photograph
Copyright © Somerset House By Kevin Meredith

Page 193 | Photograph
Copyright © Melinda Stevens

Page 195 | Photograph
Copyright © Waris Ahluwalia

Page 196-197 | Photograph
Copyright © Erdem Moralioglu

Page 199 | Photograph
Copyright © Roopal Patel

Page 200 | Photograph
Copyright © Lauren Bush Lauren

Page 202-203 | Photograph
Copyright © Hannah Cecil Gurney

Page 205 | Photograph
Copyright © Gucci Westman

Page 206-207 | Photograph
Copyright © Rosie van Cutsem and Lucia Ruck Keene

Page 209 | Photograph
Copyright © Claiborne Swanson Frank

Page 210 | Photograph
Copyright © Rachel Cecil Gurney

Page 212 | Photograph
Copyright © Lily Aldridge

Photographs of Jordan Rhodes | Copyright © Julia D'Agostino

“

ONCE A YEAR GO SOME PLACE

YOU’VE NEVER BEEN BEFORE.

Dalai Lama

ABOUT THE AUTHOR

Founder and Editor of Glimpse, Jordan Rhodes is a wife and mother to three kids, living in Greenwich, CT. Exploring the world has always been an important part of her life, but she did not want to trade in the glamour of travel once she had kids in tow, so Jordan set out to find the most stylish hotels and restaurants that also welcomed her rambunctious toddlers. Along the way, Glimpse was born so that she could share her finds, interview a variety of globetrotters and tastemakers from many different industries, and provide travel tips for discerning families, all while promoting the importance of travel as education for young kids. In 2017, Jordan founded Give A Glimpse, which uses all profits from Glimpse to help fund educational travel opportunites for students in need.

Jordan loves to answer all travel-related questions, and can be found on Instagram @jordanjrhodes and @glimpseguides.

JORDAN'S LONDON FAVORITES

My ideal day in London would begin by waking up at The Connaught and heading to a fashion exhibit at the Victoria and Albert Museum, followed by lunch at Dinings SW3 or Daphne's. I would then walk aimlessly around Chelsea before making my way back to the ERDEM and Bamford stores in Mayfair, and then edit photos over afternoon drinks at a pub, or tea at The Berkeley. Dinner would be at Scott's, followed by a night out at Annabel's, or I would see a West End show after an early meal at The Ivy. Then I would head back to The Connaught for a nightcap in the bar. The next day I would head to the countryside wearing TROY London.